D1015853

PUPPIES

A PORTRAIT OF THE ANIMAL WORLD

Marcus Schneck

TODTRI

Copyright @ 1995 by Todtri Productions Limited. All rights reserved.
No part of this publication may be reproduced, stored in a
retrieval system or transmitted in any form by any means
electronic, mechanical, photocopying or otherwise, without
first obtaining written permission of the copyright owner.

This book was designed and produced by
Todtri Productions Limited
P.O. Box 572
New York, NY 10116-0572
Fax: (212) 695-6988

ISBN 1-880908-32-8

Author: Marcus Schneck

Publisher: Robert M. Tod
Book Designer: Mark Weinberg
Photo Editor: Edward Douglas
Editors: Don Kennison, Shawna Kimber
Production Co-ordinator: Heather Weigel
DTP Associate: Jackie Skyroczky,
Typesetting: Command-O, NYC

Printed and bound in Singapore by Atomic Press Pte Ltd

PHOTO CREDITS

Photographer/Page Number

Animal Photography
Sally Anne Thompson 50, 55, 60, 70
R. T. Willbie 29, 34, 44 (bottom), 52 (top), 56-67, 58 (bottom), 62

Dembinsky Photo Associates
Dan Dempster 67
Arnout Hyde, Jr. 64

Ron Kimball 3, 5, 6, 13, 14 (top & bottom), 15 (top & bottom),
16 (top & bottom), 20, 22 (top), 24-25, 26 (bottom), 33, 37 (bottom), 39,
44 (top), 45, 47, 48 (top & bottom), 49 (bottom), 53, 59 (top), 65, 68 (bottom),
73 (bottom), 72-73, 75 (top & bottom), 76 (top & bottom), 77, 78, 79

Pets by Paulette 4, 10, 17, 18, 19, 21, 26 (top), 27, 28, 30, 31, 32,
36, 42, 52 (bottom), 54, 58 (top), 61, 66, 69

Picture Perfect USA
Robert Harding 37 (top)
Dr. Alan K. Mallams 23

Tom Stack & Associates
Barbara Von Hoffman 11 (bottom)
Brian Parker 35, 74

The Wildlife Collection
M. Boulton 43
John Guistina 8-9, 11 (top), 12 22 (bottom), 38, 40-41, 46, 49 (top), 51, 59 (bottom), 68 (top)
Martin Harvey 7, 34 (top), 71 (top)
Henry H. Holdsworth 63

INTRODUCTION

Any surface within reach of this Samoyed puppy is fair game in its constant drive to encounter new experiences and explore new realms. Samoyeds are known to have a smile as part of their natural expression.

Puppies are endowed with those characteristics that—similarly with human babies—melt our hearts and evoke feelings of love, protection, and playfulness. It was probably these feelings that led to the first human association with young dogs.

The human-dog relationship began at least 12,000 years ago, say experts, based on the discovery of a human skeleton with the bones of its hand resting on the remains of a wolflike creature similar to those from which dogs have descended. We can surmise that initial encounters occurred when dogs' wolflike ancestors were seen tracking prey, and human hunters decided to follow the animals and get in on their kill. Depending on the size of the canine pack, they then probably overpowered the pack and took the game for themselves or were able to target their own prey after the animal hunters marked the trail.

As humans continued to follow the dogs, it's likely they were led to a den where canine young were raised. And given the pups' innocent faces, limited physical size, and willingness to accept a

human 'parent', it was probably not long before people decided to keep some puppies around for amusement or as playmates for their children. Eventually those pups grew up thinking of their human family as their pack and were allowed to go along on the human hunts.

Ultimately, whilst the humans were using the animals as trackers because of their heightened senses of smell, vision, and hearing, the canines too perhaps came to realise the potential for partnership—

they could live off the spoils of the humans, who had tools that helped with the kill.

That early alliance has changed, of course, but humans and dogs still need each other. Dogs no longer roam in the wild in great numbers, and most depend on people for food and shelter. Humans no longer require dogs' senses to stalk dinner but still depend on them—as watchdogs, as companions, as helpmates, and as friends.

Sometimes people attribute to dogs human characteristics; most of the time, however, what they perceive as intelligence is in fact instinct, or canine rituals. Lhasa apsos, from Tibet, were known to perform tasks around monasteries, acting as watchdogs.

This English bulldog puppy played itself out by the time it got to the pumpkin patch. Bulldog puppies have big heads, making delivery at birth difficult.

BEGINNING OF LIFE

In this day and age, when puppies come mostly from pet shops and families are encouraged by those concerned with over-population to have their animals spayed or neutered, very few people get the opportunity to witness the birth of puppies, or even to see newborn puppies.

There are justifications for not bringing unwanted puppies into the world. However, just as puppies are born with certain instincts, there seems to be an instinct in humans that makes us curious to see puppies either being born or soon after birth. By all means, if you know someone, a breeder perhaps, whose dog is pregnant or recently gave birth, take the opportunity to peek in at them. Although their appearance will vary depending on breed and heritage, in general they will be small, quiet, helpless, and utterly irresistible.

At birth each pup is enclosed in a thin, transparent sac. The mother instinctively knows how to handle this situation, breaking the sac so the pup can breathe and eat. Then she bites off the umbilical cord and licks the pups clean, arousing them to begin breathing. She continues to lick them throughout their first few weeks, in order to stimulate waste excretion.

First Instincts

The tiny, wriggling, helpless creatures are born with their eyes and ears closed and their sense of smell barely developed. They are, however, provided with a few instincts. Relying solely on their senses of touch and taste, they wriggle around their birth area in blind search of their mother's teats.

When they find their mother's body, they shove their out-of-proportion heads along her fur until they reach a teat. They may even fall asleep in that position, relaxing there when they have filled their bellies.

During the first one or two days of its life a puppy consumes colostrum from its mother's first milk. This substance provides the protective antibodies necessary to see it through its first six to ten weeks of life whilst it develops immunities of its own.

A puppy's next instinct is to stay warm and protected. Pups are unable to control their

Following page: The experiences of these boxer puppies with their littermates in the first few weeks of life will be critical to them in their adulthood, when they will call on these early experiences for the basis of reactions to various situations.

One of a puppy's first instincts soon after birth is to find its mother's body and suckle on her teats. The next instinct is to stay warm and protected by snuggling up with its littermates. These Rhodesian Ridgebacks find comfort with their mother and the litter.

The prominent black nose on this Welsh corgi is like that of most canines— cold and wet. The moisture results when scent particles entering the nose are dissolved by nose secretions and brought into contact with the sensory cells of the nasal passages.

Few creatures convey the image of complete helplessness and innocence as does a young puppy. What mischief could these adorable King Charles spaniel puppies ever get into?

body temperature so they must be kept in a place where the temperature is approximately 27° Celsius (85° Fahrenheit). If this is not done for them, they will snuggle up with their mother and their littermates. The mother may have to leave the den area at times so the siblings will use each other for comfort. They are not advanced enough at this point to actually have social contact with one another, but they are aware that they have each other's company.

Dogs are born with a variety of other instincts—involving territory, pack behaviour, and hunting, all of which will be discussed later—but most of these do not come into play in these early weeks. At this stage of life all

they are capable of is eating and sleeping, and it is the mother's job to meet those needs and to clean, protect, and educate them.

One lesson is to teach the pups to keep their sleeping space free from excrement. For the first several weeks they will leave their wastes wherever they happen to be, including the bed, and the mother removes the mess. After a time, when they make a mistake, she will give them a shake or a shove to show her disapproval. The practical reason for this—called the 'denning instinct'—is not simply to avoid messiness but to keep the odor of dog feces and urine away from the immediate area, so predators will not be led directly to the den.

For the first several weeks of their lives puppies, like this black cocker spaniel, are nearly unable to provide for any of their own needs or defend themselves.

The mother of these Bernese mountain dogs will teach her pups not to foul their sleeping space. The practical reason for this, called the 'denning instinct', is not simply to avoid messiness but to keep odor away so that predators won't be led directly to the den.

Intelligence

As their brains grow and develop, puppies become more capable of understanding their surroundings. Most of the brain is occupied with senses and recognition, however. Very little of the puppy's brain—which throughout its life will have much less gray matter than a human's, naturally—is available for advanced ideas. Nevertheless, puppies are somewhat intelligent, as measured by how easily the animal can learn commands, tricks, routines, and other basic components of a dog's life.

Some recent evidence suggests that certain breeds are more intelligent than others. But there are those who defend their favourite breeds by noting that some only appear to be more intelligent because they have been bred to be specialised or better adapted to a particular environment, terrain, capacity, or lifestyle.

Sometimes people who do not know dogs very well attribute to them human characteristics, but most of the time what they perceive as intelligence is actually instinct, or what are known as canine rituals. Because a dog wants to remain a member of its pack, whether it be an animal or a human pack, it will learn certain routines and rules out of what it perceives as a need to remain in the good graces of those around it. Thus, what can seem like a very intelligent dog may actually be one who readily assumes a submissive or ritualistic role to retain or improve its place within its society.

A dog's senses, which are much more acute than humans', can also make a dog seem fairly intelligent and will enable the puppy to begin to master its environment. Sight and hearing, senses whose organs visibly change as the senses develop, progress by the third week, after the eyes and ears have opened.

As their brains grow and develop, puppies become more capable of understanding their surroundings. Dalmatian puppies, such as this one enjoying a festive setting, are born pure white and only gradually develop their spots.

Puppies are born with a variety of instincts involving territory, pack behaviour, and hunting; most of these will not come into play in the early weeks of this boxer's life.

13

The intelligence of puppies is measured by how easily the animal can learn commands, routines, tricks, and other basic components of a dog's life. Labrador retrievers are considered to be amongst the most intelligent breeds.

Puppies of different breeds, such as this boxer (left) and pug, have no more trouble getting along than puppies of the same breed. Boxers are particularly loving with children, and pugs are also affectionate and loving companion dogs.

Though this dachshund (right) and miniature Doberman pinscher were not littermates, they will find much in common when it comes to exploring their environment and discovering the skills they need to survive.

The world beyond its den is a big, strange, and confusing place to this beagle puppy, but it also holds a fascination that will draw it more and more away from the den and out on its own.

slightest movement of very small animals, such as insects, at more than 3 metres (10 feet), and the motion of large animals at considerable distances. Although canines do not see as much detail as humans they are able to see better in darkness. Their retinas have rods that are sensitive to low light levels, and they have a special light-reflecting layer—termed the tapetum lucidum—that makes use of available light. That reflector mechanism is what makes dogs' eyes appear to glow in the dark.

Whilst they have the extra benefit of vision in dim light, canines have long been thought to be colour blind, able to see only contrasts of black and white. But more recent studies have proved that in fact dogs can differentiate between red, yellow, blue, and green.

Canines have long been thought to be colour blind, able to see only contrasts of black and white. But more recent studies have proved that dogs, even this black-and-white bull terrier, can differentiate between red, yellow, blue, and green.

Eyesight

In general, animals whose eyes are on either side of the face, as opposed to directly in front of a flatter face, will have a field of vision of approximately 250 degrees, compared to man's 180 degrees. This makes dogs' eyes remarkably sensitive to movement. Wolves, cousins to the dog, have been known to have the capacity to detect even the

Hearing

The puppy's ears, too, as they develop fully, will be much more sensitive than humans'. A sound that a man can barely hear at 4 metres (13 feet), a dog can hear at more than 24 metres (80 feet). Wolves have been known to respond to howling from as far away as 5 kilometres (3 miles). Canines can also hear high-pitched sounds that are inaudible to humans.

Puppies are born with their eyes and ears closed, but vision and hearing begin to develop by about the third week of life. This group of puppies is clearly alert to all sights and sounds.

A sound that a man can barely hear at 4 metres (13 feet), a dog can hear at more than 24 metres (80 feet). Canines can also hear high-pitched sounds that are inaudible to humans. Size of the ears makes no difference in hearing capacity, however, so this Cardigan corgi cannot necessarily hear any better than other breeds.

The Shar-Pei is the result of cross-breeding, followed by inbreeding. It may be a descendant of the chow chow, but the only clear link between the two breeds is their purple tongue.

This basset hound's olfactory sense is many times more sensitive than a human's. The portion of a dog's brain that controls powers of smell is approximately forty times the size of that in man.

Sense of Smell

More important, however, is the puppy's sense of smell. Some experts say a dog's olfactory powers are a million times more sensitive than a man's; others stop at five hundred times the sensitivity. Even the latter seems extreme enough. In any case, the portion of a dog's brain that controls sense of smell is approximately forty times the size of that in a human's. Wolves have been known to detect their own kind from as far away as 2.5 kilometres (1.5 miles).

From birth, puppies possess what many will always joke about: a wet, cold nose. This, too, has a purpose. Scent particles entering the nose are dissolved by nose secretions and brought into contact with the sensory cells of the nasal passages.

Whilst dogs are basically nose breathers, mouth breathing becomes much more important to them during hot weather and after exertion. Some short-nosed breeds, however, have difficulty breathing through the mouth because of compressed nasal passages as a result of too much selective breeding.

Tongues and Taste

Dogs also have a well-developed sense of taste, but their tongues are more closely identified with their role in maintaining body temperature. Although dogs have sweat glands throughout the body, they also cool themselves by panting, which moves air over their wet tongue. The sweat glands manufacture a secretion that produces a dog's personal odor and, on the paws, helps to keep the walking surface soft. Dogs' coats also provide an insulating layer against heat.

Touch

A dog's sense of touch is not known to be much different than that in humans. The most sensitive parts are the front of the nose, the tongue, the lips, and the paw pads. In addition, dogs have whiskers near the lips and above the eyes that are rather sensitive and useful in protecting these areas.

Each puppy develops at its own rate and within its own inherent personality. For some, like these boxer puppies, exploration of the world beyond the den becomes a priority much earlier than for others.

This rottweiler puppy is panting as a necessary bodily function. Although dogs have sweat glands throughout their body they cool themselves by panting as well, which moves air over their wet tongue.

The dog's muscles are the largest organs in the body and vary little between breeds, although working dogs naturally get more use out of theirs than house dogs. This Welsh corgi's basic body structure allows for bursts of speed as well as for endurance as a pack hunter.

Though born without teeth, this cocker spaniel puppy has learnt to use its youthful temporary teeth, which will eventually be replaced by the sixth month with forty-two permanent teeth. The bite pattern will vary slightly amongst breeds.

Teeth

Puppies are born without teeth, which are something that will come to mean a great deal to them—for chewing, hunting, ripping, and playing. Like humans, they get two sets of teeth. Their temporary teeth grow in stages, beginning at about three weeks and normally ending by the fifth week.

Those teeth serve the purpose until the fourth to sixth month, when a puppy's forty-two permanent teeth push in. By the seventh month each side of the upper jaw will have three incisors, one canine tooth, four premolars, and two molars. The lower jaw holds nearly the same but has three molars instead of two. The bite pattern will vary slightly by the breed.

Overall, puppies are designed to be carnivorous, and are able to chase, attack, and kill prey. Their teeth are carnassial, but they have retained a few molar teeth for chewing and grinding.

Body Structure

The muscles are the largest organs in the dog's body and vary little between breeds, although working dogs naturally get more use out of theirs than house dogs. The husky, for example, can pull a load of twice its weight all day at up to 5 kilometres per hour (3 miles per hour). Basically, a dog's body structure allows for bursts of speed as well as for endurance as a pack hunter.

Puppies can be trained to jump and climb, too, but they will never be as good as cats at these skills, mainly because dogs can't control their claws or twist their legs in the same way as do cats.

All dogs are digitigrade, meaning they walk on their 'toes', unlike humans who walk on the soles of their feet. Dogs have four toes with claws; there is also a fifth claw on the inside of each foot, which does not come into contact with the ground, and a sixth toe—without the claw—on the back of each front leg. These are remnants from dogs' ancestors and have no use today.

Like all puppies, beagles should be exercised every day. Beagles are specialised for hunting and have been known to let their instincts take over when they smell game.

Gradually this English cocker spaniel puppy begins to take more of an interest in life beyond the nest, although its mother will remain a central figure for many weeks.

Because of its small size, the Shetland sheepdog is commonly mistaken for a rough collie puppy, especially since it was once known as the miniature collie. The Shetland is compact and can live in small spaces.

Reproductive Organs

The male puppy is easily distinguished from the female by his genitals; the penis and testes lie on the underside of the abdomen just between his back legs. The testes should be fully descended by about two weeks of age. As the puppy grows, fat may make them difficult to notice again until about the four-month mark.

Unless an owner plans to breed a dog, removal of the reproductive organs is usually recommended during puppyhood—for birth control, to prevent some health problems in old age, and in some cases, to tone down an aggressive personality. Males are neutered, which is essentially a castration procedure.

If a female is not spayed—a procedure in which her ovaries and uterus are removed—she will probably have her first 'season' or 'heat' between the ages of six months and a year. The smaller the breed the sooner the cycle, which can be as early as three months; the larger breeds have longer cycles, some up to two years.

A young female technically reaches maturity when her bones stop growing, which is between ten months and a year. But to assure her healthy puppies it is best to wait until she has one normal heat before breeding her. Males can be tried beginning at about ten months of age.

Two Chihuahua puppies can easily fit inside just about any hat. Although some adult Chihuahuas weigh as much as 2.5 kilogrammes (6 pounds), some weigh as little as 1 kilogramme (2 pounds), making them the smallest dogs in the world.

This Cardigan corgi puppy needs lots of rest between bouts of play, exercise, and learning. Although puppies prefer a comfortable sleeping space, they may become tired suddenly and settle down wherever they happen to be.

DISCOVERING THE WORLD

By the end of the second week, after the eyes and ears have opened, a puppy goes from helpless nestling to bouncing, frisky puppy and begins to discover the world around it. During the third week it begins to have some reactions to events in its environment and some desire to explore. Periodically, when the mother leaves the den, the puppies may try to follow.

The pup doesn't have a lot of confidence yet, and any threatening encounters will result in it reacting submissively, which at this stage means dropping on its back and exposing its throat. Because the pup has in a sense given up, the aggression is suppressed.

Starting in the fourth week the pup gains some security, its physical movements become more adept, and it learns to master its voice, its tail, and other mental skills. It now starts to express itself with voice and tail movements and will play with its littermates.

This is the phase when imprinting is accomplished, which is why humans usually pick up a new puppy around this time. At this point puppies learn to follow a 'mother' that they will accept for the rest of their lives. Other things learnt at this time regarding its environment and rituals will stay with the puppy for the rest of its life. A puppy that has no human interaction during this stage may find it difficult later to become part of a human family.

Beyond the Litter

Between the eighth and twelfth weeks, play becomes the most important thing in a pup's life. Most likely, if they are domestic dogs, they are members of human families, who are probably attempting to housetrain them and teach them various behaviours and skills.

During their third week puppies begin to display some reactions to events in their environment, and some will desire to explore. When the mother periodically leaves the den, these Shetland sheepdog puppies may try to follow.

During the imprinting phase puppies learn to follow a 'mother' that they will continue to follow for the rest of their lives if they can. Most likely this golden retriever puppy will leave its own mother and look upon a human mother-figure as the centre of its world.

In the early stages puppies don't have a lot of confidence, so threatening encounters will result in the pup reacting submissively, dropping onto its back and exposing its throat. Because the dachshund pup has given up, the aggression is suppressed.

Between the eighth and twelfth weeks, play becomes the most important thing. Plenty of exercise is essential for this golden retriever puppy, whose breed is prized as a family and companion pet.

To do this effectively pet owners will need to make learning fun, something like play. It is also at this stage that the pups learn to tell the difference between fun and serious actions.

If the pup is still with the litter, it learns about how to get along later in life by fighting with its littermates—attacking, defending, getting its own way, and reconciling after the tussle. Pups in human families also tend to do this, but with their owners. The pup learns to test how far it can go in any situation.

By the third or fourth month the pup has a fairly good understanding of its situation, its rank in the pack (to be discussed later), and the extent of its physical strength. At this stage a pup should be allowed to meet other dogs so it can familiarise itself with the social etiquette that dogs require. Soon it will lose its 'baby smell', an odor that allows it special protection up to this point from other dogs.

If pups are still in the litter by the eighth to twelfth week they are learning how to get along later in life by fighting with their littermates—attacking, defending, and reconciling. These otter hound puppies are learning how far they can go in any situation.

The eyes and ears of these beagle puppies have been open for some time. By the end of their second week they went from helpless nestlings to bouncing, frisky puppies.

To successfully wean a pup, a mother may become aggressive toward it, nudging it and walking away or even carrying it to a place outside of its normal range. This Rhodesian Ridgeback puppy will get the message after a few incidents of this kind.

and then leaving it there. Most pups get the message after a few incidents like this.

She will also feed them small amounts of her own regurgitated food. If the pup does not eat this she herself may eat it again, or store it for later to keep the den tidy.

Weaning

In the early weeks puppies feed from their mother's teats at least several times a day. They grow rapidly and need almost constant nourishment to fuel their progress.

In the wild after about six weeks a wolf mother begins to wean its pups from milk to more solid food. By that time the pups have all their primary teeth and are capable of some chewing functions.

To perform the actual weaning, a mother may become aggressive toward a pup that continues to come to the teats, nudging it away or removing herself, or even carrying the pup to a place outside of its normal range

Feeding

In the human home a puppy will most likely be offered a variety of commercial puppy chow, usually moistened with water or milk. Most veterinarians recommend feeding at least twice a day, or even up to four times per day for a very young puppy just being weaned. The daily allowance should be divided by the number of feedings, so a pup isn't getting more than one day's portion per day.

Some breeders and new puppy owners concoct special mixtures of cereal and cow's milk, followed by scraped meat or special soft meat blends. But most veterinarians today recommend one or more of the brand-name puppy food products available in the grocery store and pet shop. Generally, these consist of dried pellets made from meat, cereal, vegetable, and other food products.

Whilst soft food is sanctioned for the first several weeks, a move to crunchy food is sometimes recommended in later weeks for healthy teeth and gums, and to facilitate housetraining.

By about twelve weeks puppies that are being fed more than twice a day will lose interest in one or more of the feedings. At this time they can be cut to three feedings a

In the early weeks puppies feed from their mother's teats at least several times a day. They grow rapidly and need almost constant nourishment to fuel the progress.

This seven-week-old golden retriever pup, once weaned, should be fed a commercial puppy food at least twice a day. The daily allowance should be divided by the number of feedings so a pup isn't getting more than one day's portion per day.

day until about six months of age and then two feedings a day until nine months. Some owners prefer to cut down to one feeding per day but, if circumstances permit, two is advisable into adulthood.

Establishing Territory

In the wild, canines roam together in areas of land that they come to think of as their own. Domestic dogs, too, claim certain areas as their territory. Just as humans draw boundary lines with regard to their homes, yards, and even parking spaces, dogs select areas to call their own.

A new puppy should be able to feel that its bed area, as well as its feeding area and maybe some other space, like a play area, is its own. Its own odor from frequenting these places will be enough to make it feel at home.

Like all domestic dogs, this cavalier King Charles spaniel pup claims certain areas as its territory, just as humans draw boundary lines with regard to their homes and yards.

These bloodhound puppies are able to feel that their bed area is their own because their personal odors are prominent there. They should feel the same about their feeding area and maybe some other places, such as where they play.

Trees are amongst the targets for urination when a puppy begins to feel the need to designate its territory. These scent markings, because of special glands that add individual odors, alert other dogs to the fact that this is another's area.

A strange dog approaching this beagle puppy will enter the area slowly and be greeted by stares and hostile body language. The stranger will lower its head, droop its tail, and avoid eye contact.

Outside, however, the pup will need to mark boundaries with squirts of urine. In other words, after having followed its human owner around the property a few times and having learnt where it is expected to leave wastes and to play, the young dog feels the need to designate these areas again and again in this manner. Prime targets would be trees, poles, high plants, or just certain flat areas if nothing else is available.

These scent markings—due to special glands that add individual odors—alert other dogs to the fact that the area is one dog's territory. They become the equivalent of a dog's 'calling card'.

Canine pups are not born with this instinct. After the first several months, when they are able to leave the nest, their mother leads them out of the den and they learn to excrete wastes in a favoured spot. From this point on they show a great deal of interest in their own and other dogs' waste as a way of sniffing out and marking territory.

Whilst dogs rarely travel in groups in domestic situations, dogs in the wild travel in packs and have certain procedures in order to deal with intruders on established territory.

Communication

An approaching stranger enters the established area slowly and is greeted by stares and hostile body language. Hairs on the back are raised, the tail extends horizontally. The stranger lowers its head, droops its tail, and turns its head away, avoiding eye contact. As pack members approach, it lies down and rolls over with its belly and feet up, open for inspection.

The intruder knows that to be accepted it must appear to be submissive and puppylike. Any gesture of aggression will result in a fight, which usually ends unfavourably for the newcomer.

This is one example of how submissive

behaviour is used in dog communication. The first obvious example of this is when a pup lies on its back allowing its mother to cleanse it. Submission is also evident when a pup approaches its mother to beg for food or milk. Adult dogs are also expected to display submission if challenged by a higher-ranking member of the pack.

During a pup's first few weeks with its mother and littermates it learns this and other basics of communication. It is quite helpful for dog owners to learn the language too, so that they know what their puppy is trying to communicate when they bring it home as a member of the family.

Prior to about the fourth week of life puppies are likely to do no more than whimper, if anything, with their voices and have no real concept of communicating in any other way. Whimpering or whining is used as a means for the pups to alert mothers, or the human substitutes, that they want some-

Puppies need to be allowed to meet with other dogs so they can familiarise themselves with the social etiquette that dogs require.

Following page:
To train puppies—housetraining and various skills and behaviours—learning needs to seem like fun. This puppy is learning the difference between fun and serious actions.

thing. By the seventh week puppies learn to use their voices and tails to express themselves. Over time they come to acquire skills that involve facial expressions and other body movements.

Puppies are not yet prone to actual fighting so what sounds like a growl in a puppy is more likely a play noise. Later on growling should be taken more seriously, alerting one perhaps to stop doing whatever he or she is doing or to keep oneself at a distance.

Growling may be a sign that a dog sees itself as the individual in charge. If a growling dog is higher-ranking in the dog hierarchy, the lower-ranking dog will be expected to back down. If it does not, a fight could ensue.

Although barking is usually more annoying to humans because it is heard more frequently, it is actually a less menacing form of communication. Most dogs bark to alert other dogs or humans to the idea that something is amiss, and also to express excitement whilst at play.

Barking, although more annoying than growling, is actually less menacing, even when it comes from a larger breed like this boxer. It is primarily a means to alert others about something or to express excitement.

Prior to about the fourth week, these cocker spaniel puppies are likely to do no more than whimper, if anything, in attempting to vocalise; they have no real concept of communicating in any other way as yet.

Submission is evident as these white German shepherd puppies approach their mother to beg for food or milk. Adult dogs are also expected to show submission if challenged by a higher-ranking member of the pack.

Starting in the fourth week, puppies' physical movements become more adept and they learn to master their voice, tail, and other physical and mental skills. These Welsh corgi and Norfolk terrier pups have begun to express themselves with voice and tail movements.

Body Language

At the beginning of life puppies barely know they have tails. But by the time they start observing the entertainment possibilities in each other's tails, they also begin noticing what other pups mean by various tail movements and learn to control their own in the same ways. Tail signals vary by breed, of course, because of the various sizes and shapes of dog tails. Generally, though, a tail low and between the legs is a sign of fear; a tail pointing straight up connotes excitement; a tail sticking out horizontally relates contentment.

A dog's face also contributes to communication by utilising nose wrinkling, blinking, raising of the upper lip, and bending the ears.

Ears are a good indicator that a dog wants to communicate, especially in breeds with raised ears: erect usually means alertness or self-confidence; pointed ears relate to noise in the indicated direction; ears lying flat usually denote uncertainty, or if accompanied by growling, mean aggression.

Puppies can be observed kneading their mother's teats to stimulate the flow of milk. Grown dogs may extend their paws forward when they want something as a carryover of this action. Combined with a treat in sight, this quite easily allows most dogs to learn to 'shake' to ask for things.

The adorable puppy that owners so want to get to know may not look much at all like its wolf ancestors. But the way dogs greet with noises and body language is a direct carryover from their ancestors, so much so that it is sometimes called the 'wolf greeting'. This meet-and-greet ritual, done between friendly dogs, usually of the same pack, consists mainly of licking and nipping at one another's nose. Knowing how this works helps an owner understand why dogs always insist on 'kissing' members of the family, especially when returning to the home.

If the dogs are not on friendly terms they prick up their ears, wag their tails, sniff, and bark. If one growls there is the possibility of a fight, because growling, as noted, is a threatening vocalisation.

Dogs tend to sniff mainly at the perineal area, where the scent glands are located. They secrete fluid that serves as a kind of identity card in the feces. Fluid from these glands may also indicate a highly emotional state, such as fright. By raising or lowering its tail, the dog can unmask or mask the odor from these glands.

The way these miniature schnauzers greet each other with noises and body language is called the 'wolf greeting'. It consists mainly of licking and nipping at one another's nose.

ELEMENTS OF PLAY

Although humans feel that their puppy is a part of their family, he is also part of a larger family, that of canines, which includes the wild wolf. As part of that ancestry a pup's instincts will make him feel like he is part of your 'pack'.

Pack and Hunting Instincts

A pack is a group of animals that live together, each dependent on the others for survival. In the wild the pack supplies protection, companionship, mates, baby-sitters for the young, and hunting partners. It may not seem that this would mean a lot to your puppy, but as it grows you will see that instinct actually drives everything he does.

Each pack has one leader, usually the most dominant male. He calls all the shots, and everybody else ranks beneath him and must submit to him. The leader is often the only male to mate, probably with the dominant or alpha female. Because the leader and his mate are the strongest, they will produce strong,

Although this Bernese mountain dog has been adopted by a human family, it is by nature a member of the canine family, which includes the wild wolf. With that ancestry come instincts that make it feel comfortable as part of a pack.

These rottweiler puppies are a pack, a group of animals that live together, each dependent on the others for survival. In the wild the pack supplies protection, companionship, mates, baby-sitters for the young, and hunting partners.

Play is a daily occurrence in a dog pack. Pups play with each other almost from the day they can move, rolling and tumbling together, and later chasing and fighting over objects.

Puppies that have grown up in the same pack engage in endless games of tag and bouts of wrestling, with no attempt to use their powerful jaws in harmful biting. Occasionally, the competitors growl or bark softly in excitement.

When this beagle pup comes into a human family, that family takes the place of the pack. An owner provides it with shelter, food, protection, care, and play, acting as its mother and leader.

Canines are pack animals grouped together to ease the hunting task. They are not fast enough to outrun some prey, so they join up to circle and attack. This English springer spaniel is running with pack instincts underlying the behaviour.

healthy offspring. And because no one else is breeding, there won't be too many mouths to feed. When male and female leaders have pups the female becomes the leader of the entire pack until her pups are old enough to travel and hunt with the pack.

Hunting is the primary reason wolves and dogs are pack animals. They are not fast enough to outrun some prey, so they hunt together and circle the prey before attacking, leaving no open space to which it can run.

Once the kill is accomplished, the leader is the first to eat. All the wolves gather around the kill, and if the prey is small some of the lower-ranking members may have to wait until higher-ranking members are satisfied and move away.

Because the pack takes care of those who cannot take care of themselves, older wolves are given food if unable to obtain their own. The leader of the pack also takes food to his mate whilst she is raising the pups in the den. Pups are fed by the mother as well as by other adults in the group. They will lick food from the adults' lips, and sometimes the adults regurgitate food for them.

After the kill the pack rests awhile and may spend some time playing. If there is more food in the area, the pack may stay

After the kill the pack rests awhile and may spend some time playing, like these Norfolk terrier and Pembroke Welsh corgi puppies. If there is more food in the area, the pack may stay and make the area a home base.

Each pack has one leader, usually the most dominant male. Perhaps this German shepherd calls all the shots, and if he does, everybody else ranks beneath him and must submit to him.

Puppies like to retrieve things because of an instinct to bring home a kill after a hunt in the wild. Throw a light object like a ball or a stick, tell it to fetch, and show the pup where it is if necessary. Be sure to reward the puppy with affection or a treat.

Dogs tend to walk one step behind you when moving through the house or outside, because in the wild they would walk single file behind their leader out on a hunting expedition, in order to keep sight of each other and to use the same pawprints for ease and security.

and make the area a home base. The leader will determine when and if the pack moves on. If some members have been separated from the pack during hunting or play, the wolves will howl to gather the pack together again.

The leader will retain his position until he is unseated by a stronger, more intelligent member or until he dies. In the case of the leader's death, there will probably be some fighting amongst the higher-ranking males to determine a new leader.

Substitute Pack

When a dog comes into a human family, that family takes the place of the pack. Like a mother and leader, they provide the animal with shelter and food, protect it from harm,

keep it healthy, play with it, and maybe even provide a mate and help take care of the resulting young.

The puppy assumes it will be taken care of, but if it sees that the owner/leader is not acting in an appropriate manner, the pup attempts to take charge. This is where behaviour problems begin. If an owner takes charge it will instinctively fall into a submissive role. Owners cannot assume that they are showing their dogs the best kind of love by allowing them to do whatever they please.

If they have come to accept you as leader they will welcome the decisions you make for them and the order you bring to their lives. In fact most of pack life is devoted to reinforcing each animal's particular position in the pack.

'I'll follow you anywhere, just take me along', is the message sent by this shih tzu, all set to go in a bike basket. Having fun and belonging to the pack are life's main criteria for these companion dogs.

Play in the Wild

In the wild a wolf pack's play is a daily occurrence amongst most members of the pack. Pups play with each other almost from the day they can move, rolling and tumbling together, and later chasing and fighting one another. Play serves as a training tool, sharpening skills, reactions, and interpretations of each other's signals. This keeps them safe and serves to teach them good hunting tactics. Wolves play all their lives, even into old age, because they take on the responsibility of teaching the young. Play also serves to keep them fit and hones predation skills between kills.

Individuals that have grown up in the same pack engage in endless games of tag and bouts of wrestling with no attempt to use their powerful jaws in harmful biting. One wolf may seize another by the scruff of the neck or try to get hold of the other's jaw as they lunge at one another with mouths wide open. These sessions of rough play are almost silent, but occasionally the competitors growl or bark softly in excitement.

A true growl is a final warning to move off. A mother may produce it if playful youngsters come too close to her small pups. A few sharp barks, loud and clear, stop every wolf, no matter what it is doing, and cause it to listen alertly and discover what the danger is. A howl, particularly at night, is a sign that all is well but that strangers should stay away— beyond hearing distance. Each wolf adds its own personal harmonics whilst howling, which other wolves of the pack will recognise.

Play becomes more grown up by a pup's third or fourth month because it learns that to defend its rights it must use some intelligence as well as physical strength.

Following page: Tugging displays a puppy's natural inclination to fight. Be sure they don't take this game too seriously. Stop the game if you have to, using the 'Release' command.

These Australian terrier pups will begin to learn specific practises from their littermates during playful tussles consisting of growling, nipping, and chasing. The pups of this breed are born black and change colour after two or three months.

Puppies engage in play with other puppies by about the fourth week. By the eighth week these chows—a rough coat at left and a smooth coat at right—are eager to learn, as long as everything is taught as if it is a game.

Play serves as training time for these springer spaniels, sharpening skills, reactions, and interpretations of each other's signals. This keeps them safe and teaches them good hunting tactics.

What exactly is behind this log? This keeshond puppy is planning on finding out. Keeshonds are good swimmers and for years were the dog-of-all-jobs on Dutch boats.

The senses of this Labrador retriever are as honed as if they were vitally needed in order to track and sense game; it hears, sees, and smells things, but it no longer has to track and attack.

Puppies—when not sleeping—are always ready for play. Playfulness shines in the eyes of these cocker spaniel puppies. Whatever opportunity presents itself, they're ready to take part.

Play at Home

Domestic dogs have little chance for hunting or socialising with other dogs, but they still have the instincts naturally associated with them.

Dogs tend to walk one step behind an owner when moving through the house or outside, which can get to be annoying if you stop too quickly. They are doing this because in the wild they would walk single file behind the leader out on a hunting expedition in order to keep sight of each other, as well as to utilise the same pawprints for ease and security in traveling.

Dogs have certain rendezvous sites around the house and yard that they check periodically for interesting odors. Some dogs have been known to place their toys or bone-treats at these locations. This too is a carryover from the wild, when they would have rendezvous sites from which they knew they'd have a good chance of finding game.

Dogs that spend a lot of time outdoors may

Play for this griffon puppy has become more mature than in the early weeks of its life. It has learned that to defend its rights some intelligence as well as physical strength must be used

A basset hound puppy checks one of the rendezvous sites around the house and yard that it inspects regularly for interesting odors. This ritual is a carryover from the wild, when dogs would secure favoured places where there was a good chance of finding game.

even go through the motions of hunting down and catching prey, giving a rabbit or squirrel a good run but abandoning the chase before the final kill. Another manifestation of the hunting instinct may be the chasing of cars, motorcycles, and bikes.

These same elements come into bear when a dog plays. It does not need to hunt for its food or practise techniques with other dogs, but it still has the instincts to do so. Thus, most dogs are quite willing to enter a game of chase or tugging. In order to temper instincts it is wise to exercise the dog daily and to find some time for one-on-one play, which can be combined with training and teaching tricks.

Using toys to play with the dog will make him associate the toys with pleasant times. Throw a light object like a ball or a stick and tell him to fetch, showing where it is if necessary. Be sure to reward the puppy with affection or a treat. If you give it the toy when you go out it won't be as lonely, and will probably be more prone to playing on its own.

Capturing prey is a dog's instinctual motive when, for instance, it jumps up to catch a flying Frisbee. Honing scenting skills is the underlying activity when looking for something, like meat, that he can smell but cannot see. Similarly, tugging fits into the dog's natural inclination to fight. Be sure the dog doesn't take this too seriously and stop the game and correct this if it does.

If you bring a puppy home that has spent enough time with a litter, it is likely it will have learnt the correct attitude for play and the satisfactions that entails.

Giving toys to a puppy will make it associate the toys with pleasant times. If you give your new dog a toy when you go out, it won't be as lonely and will probably play on its own.

No possible source of play is overlooked by puppies. Some colourful flowers have caught the eye and nose of this golden retriever puppy.

PUPPY SELECTION AND CARE

The idea of bringing home a cuddly, adorable puppy to amuse and keep the family company, teach the kids responsibility, or eventually scare off intruders may seem very appealing. These are the positive aspects of embracing a puppy.

Owning a puppy, however, eventually leads to owning an adult dog, and as the puppy grows so can the problems. Anyone taking in a puppy should be prepared to offer at least a ten-year commitment; this is not of course like a sweater that you can return if you find it doesn't fit as well as you thought. So before you take the plunge, and maybe have to sever a relationship, it's wise to consider all the factors.

Make sure everyone in the household wants to embark on a relationship with a puppy. Who will take care of it? Can you afford food and equipment? Can you afford the veterinarian bills, for routine vaccinations and checkups as well as for emergencies? Do you have time to exercise the pup, to train and play with it? Once you *have* decided you want a dog, you must now decide what kind you want.

What Kind of Puppy?

Size should be a major consideration. Do you have enough room for a large dog? Will a small dog always be underfoot in your living area? Whether your choice is large or small, try to find out enough about your dog's heritage to understand how big it will grow.

You also need to decide if you want a purebred dog or a mutt (mixed breed). If you want to show your dog, you will need a purebred. A purebred dog will have certain inherited traits and characteristics, so you can be fairly certain as to how it will look and what its

Whether you choose a small dog the size of this toy poodle or something larger like a Great Dane, get to know your puppy's heritage to understand just how big it will grow.

Be sure to teach children how to handle a puppy so good times like this fishing expedition can be shared by both kids and dog. Be careful about leaving a dog and a young child alone together, because even a good-natured dog can overreact to a child's aggressiveness.

temperament might be when it's grown.

There are more than three hundred dog breeds in the world. The largest of these is the Irish wolfhound, which can measure as much as 80 to 90 centimetres (32 to 36 inches) at the withers. At the other end of the spectrum is the Chihuahua, which may be no more than 15 centimetres (6 inches) tall.

Breeds of dogs are also categorised into groups: sporting dogs, which have extraordinary instincts in the outdoors; hounds, known for their keen tracking powers; working dogs, bred to perform tasks such as guarding and pulling; terriers, generally spirited and energetic; toy dogs, ideal apartment dogs because of their small size; non-sporting dogs, a varied collection of appearances and personalities; and herding dogs, which have the ability to control the movement of other animals.

Although these are grouped mainly by function, your local kennel club can expand on the various traits of breeds within those groups. For example, if you want a puppy that will grow into a dog especially good with children, you could narrow your search quickly by choosing from breeds that are noted for that characteristic. You could then choose from amongst other traits within those breeds to match your family's needs.

Maybe a mutt is more your style. However, the mutt puppy you acquire may not grow exactly into the dog you thought it would. The previous owner may tell you it is a mix of certain breeds, but since no one knows its heritage for sure you may find out differently as the puppy grows.

Another consideration is the age of the dog. Can you handle the growth and training periods of a puppy, or might you be happier with an older dog that is already trained and socialised?

Male or Female?

You also need to decide if you want a male or a female. Various myths are circulated regarding both. For example: a female will become more attached to a male owner than to a female owner; or, male dogs are less trouble. These are not rational considerations. A male, however, will do more marking of territory with urine, and a female, on the other hand, will go into heat twice a year.

Both males and females have reactions to the female's heat: the female may be disobe-

Most new dog owners prefer to begin their association with a very young puppy, but they must be aware that the younger dog will require more care and attention.

Some families adopt a dog to teach children responsibility. Here, a brother and sister do their part by giving the family dog a bath. Depending on the breed, baths, in addition to daily grooming, are needed on a regular basis.

Select a puppy that looks healthy, whose surroundings are clean, who is alert and curious, and who is weaned from milk. Do not overlook any signs of backwardness or disease.

This mixed-breed puppy will be acceptable to those who don't feel any compulsion to show a dog or require a pedigree for it in hand. If you know the heritage of your mutt, you can to some degree figure out what characteristics it may grow up to have.

dient and run off in search of a male; some males cannot resist the scent of a female in heat. Any problems associated with heat can be resolved, as noted, by neutering or spaying. Even if you aren't concerned about these potential problems, it is recommended that puppies be fixed—if you do not plan on breeding them—to avoid more unwanted dogs in the world.

A new owner can do his or her part to alleviate this situation by selecting the puppy from an animal shelter. Most charge a nominal fee for neutering or spaying. If you want a purebred, however, you usually must buy from a pet shop, a breeder, or someone you know. The seller should provide you with the necessary papers.

Your New Puppy

Select a puppy that looks healthy. It should not have a runny nose, watery eyes, a dull coat, or a potbelly; be too thin, have a fever,

or seem weak or ill. Check its ears for mites and infection, and to make sure it can hear. Check its mouth to make sure that its gums and teeth are healthy. Its surroundings should be clean and its littermates free of disease as well.

The pup should seem alert and curious. Do not choose one that seems shy or awkward, snappy or bad-tempered. It should be comfortable around humans and willing to come when you bend down to it. It helps if it appears to be slightly aggressive toward its littermates. To leave the litter, it should be weaned from milk and already eating solid food.

Puppies have matured enough to leave their mother by about six to eight weeks of age. Before that they may not be strong enough to survive on their own, and they may not have spent enough time in the 'den' with their littermates to have acquired the denning instinct necessary for proper training outside the litter.

Because this Tibetan spaniel is a purebred it will be amongst those you can choose if you want a show dog. Purebred dogs are usually obtained from breeders.

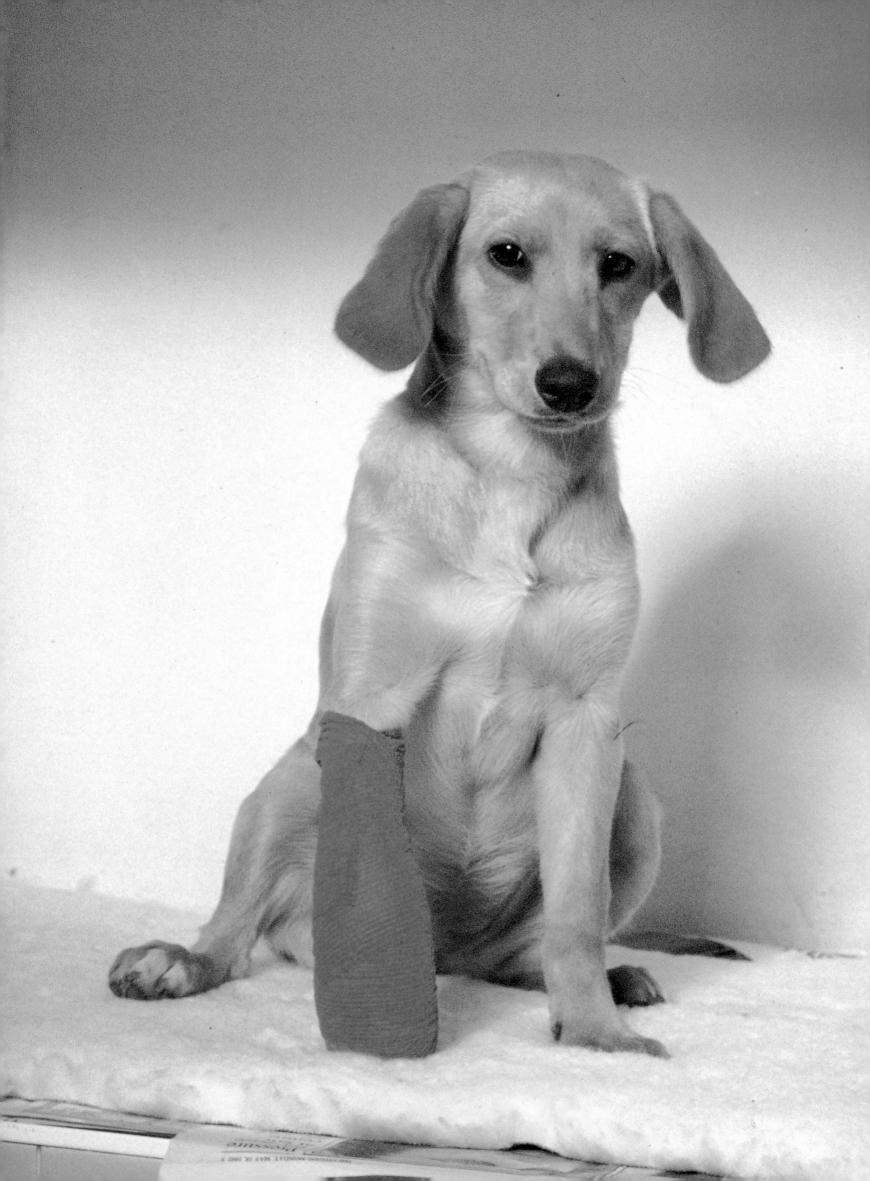

A New Home

When you take the puppy home—in a crate for safety—don't overwhelm it by placing it with too many people. Take a few minutes at once to show the puppy its sleeping area, and give it time to examine everything in peace. Don't alarm it with loud noises; talk softly and pet it. It will soon get the idea that this is its new home. Then gradually introduce the puppy to other members of the family.

The puppy's bed should be in a draft-free area that is out of the lane of traffic. Because the pup will have accidents, a non-carpeted area is preferred, as is one that can be closed off from the rest of the house. The bed might be a wooden box, a basket, or a box lined with a rug or blanket. Crates made for carrying dogs in cars make ideal beds because they can be latched and may make the dog feel very secure. They also lend themselves to house-training because of the denning instinct.

The puppy should be shown its food and water dishes and given the first meal in its new home as soon as possible. Give it about a third less than is normal for this first meal, and keep a distance while it eats.

Some owners give their dogs bones or rawhide treats when they get a little older, which corresponds to a dog's natural instincts to chew. Pups will inevitably want to chew on something, so it's wise to allow them something, or they will seek out substi-

These Rhodesian Ridgeback puppies should be at least six weeks old before leaving the litter to allow sufficient time with their mother and littermates to acquire the denning in-stinct. They should also be weaned from milk and eating solid food.

tutes, such as your shoes or furniture. The kind of rawhide treat that breaks into particles is preferred to those that just moisten and become soft, as they are less easy to choke on.

Although the pup can seem fine during the day, its first night away from the litter may be traumatic. It will be lonely and may chew or whine or cry. You might try giving it a hot-water bottle and an old-fashioned ticking clock to substitute for its mother's and litter-mates' heartbeats.

Although it is tempting to save the puppy from its lonely night, it is best to ignore it. Rescuing it from its secluded space will unin-tentionally train it to cry every night until you do so again. On the other hand, never punish the puppy for crying. And after a quiet night, by all means, praise your pup.

The puppy's bed should be in a draft-free area out of the lane of traffic, perhaps in a space that can be closed off. The bed can be a wooden box, a basket, or a box lined with a rug or blanket.

Can you afford the veteri-narian bills for this puppy, even if he is accident prone or contracts some serious disease? Along with emergency care there will be routine visits for vaccinations and checkups.

Following page: If you don't want your new beagle puppy lying in your flower garden, you should use the 'No' command for teaching such restrictions. Other useful commands are 'Release', 'Heel', 'Come', and 'OK'.

71

Bonding

Bonding is a necessary first step in training your dog. When the puppy is secure in the pack, it will be confident in your dealings with it. If it bonds with you, it will be eager to please you.

Let the puppy know that it is safe and accepted by you before you even think about rigourous training. It won't hurt to begin gentle housetraining, but it's best if you first take time to get to know your dog and allow it to explore its new home. For a while the puppy may squirm away when you reach for it, but someday it will nuzzle up to you with a head on your lap, a paw on your chest, or some sign of affection.

Bonding also involves introducing the dog to the family's routines. Let it know that there is a time to sleep, play, exercise, and eat. Allow it to keep you company throughout the day, and on outings. Get down to its level on the floor and play with it as if you are another puppy, allowing it to misbehave a little. It helps if the whole family bonds with

Although these puppies may seem fine the day they are split up and taken to different homes, their first night apart could be very traumatic. Acceptable substitutes for comfort are a hot-water bottle and a ticking clock.

the new puppy, even if it is to differing degrees. The dog will accept each relationship for what it is and look to one member of the family, usually the one who gives the orders, as the leader of its pack.

Be sure to teach children how to handle a puppy, and be careful in leaving a dog and a child alone together because even a good-natured dog can overreact to a child's aggressiveness.

Patience, a gentle touch, calm tones, reward, and praise are critical in developing a warm and affectionate long-term relationship with puppies.

When introducing a new puppy to your home, show it its food and water dishes, giving the first meal in its new home as soon as possible. Give the pup some distance whilst it gets used to its new surroundings.

Teach this Lhasa apso to lie down by saying 'Lie' and gently pulling its legs forward from a sitting position.

Don't put your puppies 'on a shelf' like these two; give your puppy care and attention every day to assure the new member of your family that it is a part of your human pack.

Training

Up until your new puppy was separated from its litter, it may have relieved itself whenever and wherever it wanted. It does not yet understand why your main goal in its life is to make sure it doesn't do this—and it will never understand if you punish it when it makes this mistake.

As soon as you bring your new charge home take it outside to relieve itself or, if you want to start with paper training, place it on some paper in its area. Give the pup the chance to relieve itself approximately every two hours: first thing in the morning, after meals, after naps, and when you see it wandering around restlessly or turning in circles while sniffing. Remember to reward it with praise each time it successfully goes outside.

The easiest way to train a puppy is to keep it in a crate most of the time. Because of its denning instinct, the pups will avoid messing their crate and wait to be taken out before they relieve themselves. Of course even this method will not work if the wait is too long. So there may at times be accidents overnight. Denning should not preclude your taking your puppy out of the crate to play.

Tell this Chihuahua puppy to 'Stay' if you want him to remain on this bench whilst you walk away. This is a difficult concept for some dogs, so be patient and keep trying.

Commands

Although you can start teaching commands to a seven-week-old puppy, you cannot realistically expect the desired results until the pup is about six months old. Successful training should be rewarded with affection and praise and/or a treat. Do not punish for unsuccessful training, but consider professional training if the dog goes months without any progress.

Get the young dog used to its collar and leash from the start. Then teach it its name, using it as the first word whenever you speak to it. Teach it to sit by holding its head up and pushing its back end down gently. To train it to lie down, gently pull its front legs forward from a sitting position.

Next tell the sitting or lying dog to 'Stay', and move slowly away. Increase the distance each day. Teach it to come to you by offering it a treat and saying the word. The treat is its reward.

'No' is useful for teaching restrictions; 'Release' for giving up precious possessions; 'OK' for release from discipline or another command; 'Down' for getting down and not jumping; and 'Heel' for walking in step. Other, more optional commands include tricks such as giving a paw (shake), rolling over, and barking on command.

Whatever you decide to teach your new puppy, do it with patience, a gentle touch, and a calm tone. The puppy will soon become a valued member of the family.

Owning this adorable Jack Russell terrier puppy will eventually lead to owning a full-grown Jack Russell terrier dog. Be sure you prepare yourself for bigger problems as well as bigger rewards.

After this pointer becomes accustomed to its collar and leash you can teach it its name and then try the 'Sit' command, holding its head up and pushing its back end down gently.

INDEX

Page numbers in **bold-face** type indicate photo captions.